I0840196

What's a Photo

Without the Story?

To my family;
past, present,
and future.

Also by Hazel Thornton:
Hung Jury: The Diary of a Menendez Juror
("20 years later" edition)
Graymalkin Media 2018

Table of Contents

Introduction
Who is this book for?

Do you have a box full of old photos and no idea what to with them? How about an intriguing family story that has never been verified or documented? Or keepsakes that might be confused for trash when you die?

I wrote this book to encourage and help you — *yes, you!* — to tell your family stories; even — *especially!* — if you are not a genealogist, or a photo organizer, or a writer.

Each part of the book includes the following sections (and more):

WHY: Why tell your stories? Why add photos to them? Why learn more about your family history? Why leave a legacy, not a burden?

HOW: These sections offer specific actions for you to take, depending on your desired goals and how much effort you want to put into meeting them.

PHOTO STORIES: I've included some of my own family photos, and the stories behind them, to inspire you to tell YOUR stories. The first one, about my bathing beauty grandma on the cover of this book, is the longest. The rest are quite short. Your stories can be as long, or as short, as you like!

Here's how YOU can participate in creating YOUR family legacy:

Low effort *(Do this if nothing else.)*

- Why not give a copy of this book to the historian, genealogist, photo keeper, or storyteller in your family? If you read it first, you'll surely gain a greater appreciation of these family members and perhaps find ways to help them preserve and share your family legacy.

Medium effort *(Your family will thank you.)*

- Take action on some of the ideas you find in this book and share your progress and results with your family!

High effort *(Ask for help if you need it.)*

- Each section of the book contains helpful resources, and Part 5 will help you become even more resourceful! When I search for something online, I most often use Google (search engine) on Firefox or Safari (web browsers). But feel free to use whatever search engine(s) and web browser(s) you prefer!

As you read, you may find yourself thinking:

But, what if I'm not:
- *A photo organizer?*
- *A genealogist?*
- *A writer?*

What if nobody's interested in my stories, or my genealogy research, or my things? Then what?

Trust me. I've worked with clients as a residential professional organizer for 15+ years (continuously); as a genealogy researcher for 30+ years (off and on); as a blogger and author; and as a member of various local and national organizing, genealogy, and historical associations and societies. And *I've never met a person who didn't have a story worth telling*. Everyone has a story, and this book will help you tell yours!

There are lots of easy ways for you to tell your family stories (Part 1) and enhance your stories with photos (Part 2). If you get curious, you can dig deeper roots and climb higher into the branches of your family tree by learning more about your ancestry (Part 3). While you're at it, why not declutter, downsize, and tell the stories of your prized possessions, too, so you can leave a legacy, not a burden (Part 4)?

Let's start with one of my own family stories. Don't worry; yours don't have to be as lengthy as this one, and the rest of the Photo Stories in this book are *much* shorter!

What's a photo without the story?

Bathing Beauty
Who took this photo? Good question!
From the estate of Archie R. Thornton Jr.

Who is this saucy young bathing beauty? Don't know? Don't care? She looks like fun, though, doesn't she?

What if you found this photo in a bin at Goodwill? Or, for sale on eBay? Would you buy it? Would you feel vaguely sad that somebody got rid of it, and then move on with your day?

What if you found her photo in your parents' stuff that you inherited, but didn't know who she was? Would you keep, or toss?

Would you try to find the story behind the photo?

Allow me to introduce you to Hazel Islery Clay Thornton, my paternal grandmother and namesake. Sadly, she died at 44, when my dad was just 16 years old. I never got the chance to know her. I had seen, when I was a child, a few photos of her as an adult. But it wasn't until recently that I discovered this photo of her younger self in an old album. It made me feel like I'd just "met" her for the first time.

There's more to Hazel's story than I will ever know, but I'm happy for the chance to know this much: She was kind. She was happy. She was fun-loving. My dad adored her, and said she sang like an angel. (I had no idea he meant that she sang *professionally*, until I found some concert ads on Newspapers.com!)

And what are names and dates without photos?

You've seen my namesake grandma's photo. Now let's look at a couple of census records.

Here is little Hazel, living with her parents and younger brother Herman, in 1910 Richmond, Virginia:

Year: 1910; Census Place: Richmond Jefferson Ward, Richmond (Independent City), Virginia; Roll: T624_1644; Page: 10B; Enumeration District: 0099; FHL microfilm: 1375657

To me, speaking as a genealogist, this U.S. Census record is almost as good as a photo — *Look, how cute! She's only 3 years old!* — but I can understand if it's not quite as meaningful to you. Also, I had the benefit of seeing the whole record, including the column headers, not just the snippet shown.

And here she is living with her husband and two children (including my dad, Archie Jr., age 6) in 1940 Los Angeles, California:

Thornton	Archie R.	Head		M	W	40	M	No	C-4	70	California
	Hazel	Wife		F	W	33	M	No	H-3	20	Virginia
	Betty Clay	Daughter	2	F	W	13	S	Yes	8	8	California
	Archie Raymond	Son	2	M	W	6	S	Yes	1	1	California

Year: 1940; Census Place: Compton, Los Angeles, California
Roll: T627_224; Page: 61A; Enumeration District: 19-110

These facts would be so much more interesting with a photo or two to go with them, wouldn't they? This one is from around 1937. Close enough!

Photo Credit:
From the estate of Archie R. Thornton Jr.

And how boring are pedigrees (ancestry charts) without photos? We can see from this one that Hazel married Archie Sr. in 1925 Los Angeles.

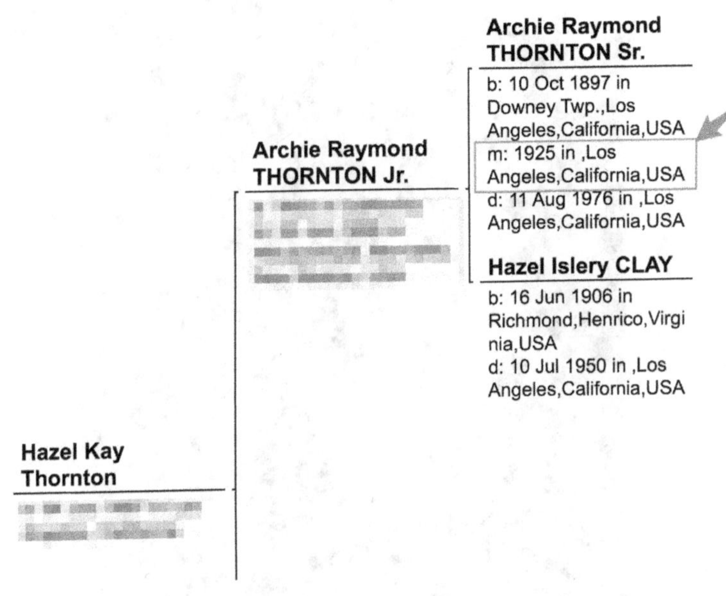

Portion of the author's pedigree chart

But, surely we can illustrate this occasion in a more compelling way…

Photo Credit:
From the estate of Archie R. Thornton Jr.

Ah, that's better! This photo goes a long way towards bringing their Jazz Age wedding day to life, doesn't it?

Digging deeper

Even though I already knew who the girl on the beach was, I still had questions — Who was she posing for? (My grandpa, maybe, when they were courting?) What beach is this? (One of the many beaches in Southern California, where they lived?) Was it a special occasion? (Their honeymoon, perhaps?) Was she staying in that hotel? (With my grandpa?)

I knew the photo was taken in the 1920s from the style of the swimsuit and headband; because of how old she looks to me (17-22); and because of her known lifespan (1906 - 1950). But was it a snapshot of her life before, or after, her 1925 marriage?

A prominent feature in the photo is the giant hotel (or is it an apartment building?) in the background. I asked my dad if he recognized it or knew anything else about the photo. He didn't. After striking out with an internet image search of existing or historic beachside hotels in Southern California (and then, worldwide), I posted the photo on Facebook and asked my friends. A couple of them thought they recognized it as the Hotel Del Mar in Santa Monica.

But I had my doubts.

The U-shaped building design and hip roof style were, indeed, quite similar. I probably could have left it at that, and nobody would have been the wiser. Even considering possible remodeling over the years, though, the window placement was slightly different, and I couldn't account for the building shown next door in the photo. There were too many architectural differences, and I really wanted to know! So, I contacted the hotel itself, and the Santa Monica Historical Society…with inconclusive results.

Eventually, I turned to Maureen Taylor, The Photo Detective. She agreed with my instinct that it was not the Hotel Del Mar. She showed me other buildings from that era with similar architecture, and led me through a series of questions: Where, exactly, did my grandparents live? (I found a map online and pinpointed their addresses, which I obtained from 1920 and 1930 census records.)

Where were the *closest* beaches, and thus the most likely ones for them to have visited? (Santa Monica and Long Beach were the straightest shots from where they lived, with many other beaches in-between.) Were they known to travel? (Not that I've heard.) Were there any other photos taken that day? (Not that I've seen.)

I did find a photo of my grandpa with my Aunt Betty at the beach when she was a child, though. She was older than my dad, but it was still the 1920s. It showed a sign in the background that read — microscopically, but clearly — *Silver Spray Pleasure Pier*. Which, at that time, according to the internet, was in Long Beach.

Photo Credit:
From the estate of Archie R. Thornton Jr.

I remembered my dad saying he had enjoyed visiting Long Beach as a child and asked him about it. He replied, "Mom used to take me to Long Beach by bus, with my little sand bucket and tiny shovel…just her and me…When I was a little older, going to The Pike was a real treat."

I changed my internet search to *beach hotel Long Beach 1920s* — and there it was! The Hotel Virginia in Long Beach!

In an article I found entitled *"The opulent rise and dismal fall of the Hotel Virginia in Long Beach"* (referring to the Great Depression), the historian noted, "The Virginia, with no hope of a national economic recovery in sight, closed its doors in October 1932, just weeks before it would've likely fallen to the Long Beach quake of '33. It was razed and the rubble was carried away from the town."

Well… no wonder my dad didn't recognize it. He wasn't born until the very same year the hotel was destroyed — 1933!

Sadly, it also indicates that he didn't spend much time with his parents looking at old photos and learning their stories. And I never saw the photo of my grandma Hazel on the beach until I was in my 60s.

So, mystery solved!

Well, much of it, anyway. We may never know who took the photo.

You might not choose to go to the lengths I did to learn more about your own mystery photos, but this book will give you lots of ideas for telling your stories however it seems most natural and fun for you.

Part 1:
Tell Your
Family Stories

Preserve your memories,
keep them well,
what you forget
you can never retell.

— Louisa May Alcott

Why tell your stories?

Are you eager to tell your stories? Great! Wait — no? What are some of the thoughts that pop into your head when I suggest it?

- *It's too hard.*
- *I'm not a writer.*
- *I don't know how or where to begin.*
- *Why bother, who cares?*
- *Yay, I can't wait to get started!*

I hope it's that last one. But I understand completely if it's not. Either way, I'll be serving up bite-sized ideas that anyone — writer or not — can easily accomplish.

Family stories can:

- Give depth and meaning to your photos.

- Make history come alive!

- Preserve family legends (rumored or proven).

- Give children a sense of belonging and help them feel more secure.

- Make us feel connected to our families, and to the world around us.

- Help us better understand our families, and ourselves.

Maybe it will help if we first think about some different kinds of stories.

Stories about yourself

Ugh! I know. This smacks of writing an autobiography, right? Enjoyable for some, perhaps, and way too much, or too personal, for others. Think about how much you enjoy hearing other people's stories, though. Is there something unique about your life, or about an experience you've had that you'd like to share, or document? What about a hobby you enjoy, or a cause you feel passionate about?

Stories about your family

If you're not keen on telling your own story just yet, try telling your parents' stories, or your grandparents', first. If they are still alive, maybe they can help you with the details. You might find that you all enjoy working on this project together! If it's too late for that, think about what you wish they'd told you, and use those ideas as the basis for learning more about them. What do you regret not asking them when you had the chance?

Once you've got a family story or two under your belt, try writing that same sort of story about yourself for your kids and grandkids; or for your distant cousins that you may never meet (who might discover them through genealogy research); or for yourself.

Stories about your ancestors

The more you know about your ancestors, the more stories you will be able to capture and preserve for future generations. Part 3 (*Dig Deeper & Climb Higher*) will help you learn more about your family tree if you are so inclined.

Stories about your photos

In this era of digital photography and smartphones, most of us have a camera in our pocket at all times. We take more photos every day than our ancestors did in their entire lifetimes! This means that we can easily end up with thousands of photos if we don't delete photo clutter on a regular basis. The more you can organize and maintain your photo collection, the less frustrated you will become when you try to find the one you want. *(See: Organize your photos)*

Meanwhile, not all photos are equally special. How is anyone going to care about yours if there are thousands of them? Or, if they don't know who's in them, or why they were meaningful to you? Part 2 *(Enhance Your Stories with Photos)* will help you curate your collection and make it more manageable.

But (you may be wondering) isn't a picture worth a thousand words?

Indeed, it is! A photo can convey so much – like the warmth of a summer day and the beauty of nature. It can evoke a time and place – but which time, exactly? And which place? A photo can portray the love between two people – but what are (or were) their names? And how are they related to you? By adding just a few more words to your own thousand-word pictures, you could transform them into something that will be cherished for generations!

Stories about your things

It can be burdensome — can't it? — to inherit someone's possessions if there are too many of them, and if you don't know what to do with them. So, why not help your loved ones out by taking photos of your special belongings, and telling the stories behind them? That's what Part 4 (*Leave a Legacy, Not a Burden*) will help you do. That way, the people important to you will know what's important, sentimental, historical, or valuable. And what isn't.

What if you don't have any stories to tell?

Oh, but you do! I haven't met anyone yet who doesn't have a story. Even if you feel ordinary, or doubt anyone would want to hear your story, I guarantee there is something unique about you and your life experience worth telling. Or perhaps you have so much to say you don't know where to begin?

If you truly don't have a story, then the story may be the mystery of why you don't have a story!

What if nobody else cares about your personal or family history?

Ah. Well, you wouldn't be alone in having that thought! *(See: What if nobody else cares?)*

It doesn't have to be perfect

In fact, let's just assume right now that your stories *won't* be perfect. But they will be a start. You don't even have to know what you're going to eventually do with them to get started.

Just remind yourself you don't have to show anyone if you don't want to. Think of whatever you create as a first draft. (Even "real" writers start with first drafts!) If you don't get it out of your head, and into a first draft, then there will be nothing for you (or others) to improve upon, right? And the stories will be lost.

As I tell my organizing clients, it's up to you whether to use my ideas as described. In some cases, they might just trigger an idea of your own that you'd like to try. Go for it!

After all, if you don't tell your stories, who will?

Are you ready to add stories to your photos?

25

Let's get started! The next section will tell you how.

How to add stories to your photos

ere are some specific actions for you to take, depending on your desired goals. You don't have to do all the things! And you certainly don't have to do them all at once. You will enjoy the journey more if you take it a step at a time. Think of it as a new hobby, rather than a one-and-done event.

Low effort *(Do this if nothing else.)*

- Start with your favorite printed photos. Jot a few cursory details on the back of the photo using the Five Ws of journalism as a guide: *Who? What? When? Where? Why?* Use an ordinary pencil (#2 or softer), or a Stabilo brand photo-safe pencil. Be sure to avoid hard pencils, and don't use an ink pen or marker that might bleed or smear). Keep the photos all together so you, or someone else, can find and enjoy them, and perhaps continue the storytelling process you have begun.

- Sit down with your older relatives and ask them questions about their lives. Such as: What do you remember about your childhood and teenage years? How did your family celebrate holidays and other special occasions? What family stories or memories were passed down to you? (For an arsenal of ideas, search online: *interviewing older family members*.) Write down the answers. Or, better yet, record the conversation. Smartphones have audio and video tools built in. And most video conferencing software (like Zoom) lets you record, so relatives don't have to live nearby to join in the fun.

- Tell your family some stories about your own favorite memories. Ask someone to take notes or record your conversation. If no one seems interested, hire a young relative or a neighbor kid to help you. Or write the stories down yourself. If you don't want to handwrite or type, you can use dictation software (Word has a built-in dictation feature) or have an audio file transcribed by a service like Rev.com.

Medium effort *(Your family will thank you.)*

- Write a story about your favorite family photo. Write what you know, and don't worry about what you don't know. Again, remember the 5-Ws of journalism: *Who* is in the photo? Do you know *who* took it? *What* else is going on? Do you know *when* and *where* it was it taken? *Why* is it important or special to you? Repeat for as many of your favorite photos as you like. Do a few each day or each week and you will end up telling a lot of stories! They can be as long, or as short, as you like.

- Give your loved ones (or yourself) a subscription to StoryWorth (an email service that asks a question about one's life every week for a year, and compiles your replies into a book), or Memorygrabber (a downloadable fill-in-the-blank life story workbook).

- Write family stories on your computer and add digital photos to them as illustrations, sort of like a holiday newsletter.

- Try writing your own obituary. Consider how you'd want to be remembered to future generations who won't have met anyone who knew you in person. (For ideas and templates, search online: *write your own obituary*.)

- Dig deeper into your family history by researching your family tree. This, too, can be done at various levels of interest. *(See Part 3: Dig Deeper and Climb Higher)*

High effort *(Ask for help if you need it.)*

- Further examine your photos for clues to additional stories. *(See: Identifying Mystery Photos)*

- Search Newspapers.com (subscription) or Chronicling America (free) for relatives in specific locations and periods of time. Depending on the size of the community, you could find news about everything from weddings and funerals to murders and birthday parties.

- Make an album of printed photos, with descriptive captions or stories, using a digital service such as Picaboo or Blurb.

- You don't have to write a book-length memoir or publish your stories to make writing them worthwhile. But you may find yourself becoming interested in doing just that. To improve your writing skills and learn about publishing options, check out local writing groups and writers' conferences in your area.

- Learn to let go of perfectionism by listening to the "Getting to Good Enough" podcast co-hosted by life coach Shannon Wilkinson and professional organizer Janine Adams. *(See: Knowledge, Inspiration & Assistance)*

- Hire a personal historian to help you tell and document your stories. *(See: Knowledge, Inspiration & Assistance)*

PHOTO STORY: Like Mother, Like Daughter

Photo credit:
Archie R. Thornton Jr.

The Photo:

A woman and a small child sitting on a lawn glider and reading books together

The Story:

Awww…I love this photo! It's my mom (left) and me (right) in July 1959 Albuquerque, as you can see from the handwritten captions that I found in Mom's old photo album. The picture captures the beginnings of a life-long love of reading instilled in me by Mom (also by Dad, the photographer). Unbeknownst to me, it was also my last month on earth as an only child! My brother Michael would be born in August.

Having seen this photo many times over the years, something only recently caught my eye — as I enlarged the photo, the inside cover of the book in my lap suddenly looked familiar. As a volunteer at my local Friends of the Library, I recognized it as a volume from a set of children's books I have priced numerous times for our monthly used book sales. Which made me wonder, "Hmm, where is that box? Is in the hall closet?"

Et voila! I still have that book! It's Volume 1, *In the Nursery,* of the *My Book House* series, published by Olive Beaupre Miller. It's even crayon-scribbled, as are most of the first pre-loved volumes of this book series for children.

(This photo also appears in my Org4life.com blog post: *Mother's Day — Gifts I Got From Mom.*)

Identifying mystery photos

Do you ever look at an old family photos and wonder, "Who are these people, anyway?"

So many people throw photos in the trash because they don't know the people in them. And the organizer in me agrees: *They're photo clutter! Toss! Don't keep!*

But the genealogist in me says — *Hold on just a minute! When was this photo taken? Whose house is this? What was the occasion? Every photo has a story. If you don't know what it is, maybe you can find out!*

If you know something about the photo…

What is your starting point?

- Where did you get the photo? Do you know who took it? Is there a date printed on the photo by the processing lab, or by a previous owner? Is there handwriting on the back? Do you see a face you recognize? Is the setting familiar?

- If the photo is in an album, or stored with other photos, are there adjacent photos to help you put it into context?

- Who *else* is in the photo? Could they, too, be related? Look for family resemblances. Consider who else was living nearby at the time the photo was probably taken. You can find out from census records. Perhaps they were visiting neighbors or relatives. Perhaps they were neighbors who were *also* relatives!

If you know nothing about the photo…

It may seem impossible to know who is in a photo if you don't recognize anyone, or anything.

- Whose house could that be? Does it resemble any of the houses in other photos you've seen?

- The older the photo, the more likely the people in it were important to the family, because they didn't take as many photos as we do today.

- Was it professionally taken? Can you find the name of the studio online?

- What style of hair, dress, jewelry, automobile, or other items do you see that would indicate a timeframe?

- Are there any landmarks or signs in the photo (such as the Silver Spray Pleasure Pier sign in my introductory story)?

- I've never been a fan of colorized photos. But sometimes colorizing or sharpening a photo, by using tools such as those provided by MyHeritage or Vivid-Pix, can bring attention to helpful details that might otherwise be missed. (Think: a pendant that your great-aunt is wearing in an old photo, which was indistinguishable in grey tones from her dress, and now you realize it's an heirloom that is still in your family, or a design you can research for dating purposes.) I used a colorized photo for the cover of this book, not so much because I got clues from it, but because it makes the image of my grandmother stand out from the background.

- Don't discard mystery photos. You never know where or when your next clue could appear!

If you need help...

- Hire Maureen Taylor, The Photo Detective, to help you investigate, or read her blog and books on the subject. *(See: Knowledge, Inspiration & Assistance)*

PHOTO STORY: Gone But Not Forgotten

Photo credit:
Janelle Thornton

The Photo:

An unusual-looking gravestone

The Story:

My great-grandmother Ethel Lee Robbins Lawrence, and her unborn child, died in the 1918 Spanish Flu pandemic, leaving my 14-year-old grandmother, Villa, to raise her three younger brothers and baby sister almost single-handedly. Villa described her father as "a drunkard and a rent-jumper" who worked seven days a week at a clay sewer pipe factory.

Imagine my surprise, upon visiting Arabia Cemetery in Mecca, Indiana, when I saw this unusual gravestone: a hand-made sculpture of a tree trunk — made from clay sewer pipes! I had previously learned that the traditional meaning of a tree trunk, in cemetery symbology, is that of being cut down in the prime of life.

The epitaph reads: "Gone but not forgotten."

(A longer version of this story appears in my Org4life.com blog post: *Our Ancestors and the 1918 Spanish Flu.*)

Part 2:
Enhance Your Stories With Photos

Photos give us the power to love people
from our past,
our present, and our future.

—Andi Tormohlen Willis,
Good Life Photo Solutions

Why add photos?

Pairing photos with stories makes the photos more meaningful and the stories more memorable.

Family Photos can:

- Make stories come alive!
- Make names and dates more interesting.
- Help solve family mysteries (and sometimes create new ones).
- Provide a window to the past.
- Intrigue us with family resemblances.

If you are the family historian, it is tempting to compile all your genealogy research into a massive pedigree chart and present it to your family, "See? Look at all of our ancestors!"

And then watch their eyes glaze over. No, they don't see, not really. They weren't as immersed as you were in the discovery process and the names and dates don't mean nearly as much to them as they do to you.

So, you write summaries of what you've learned about your ancestors, making full sentences and paragraphs out of the names, dates, and places. Then you add where they are buried, how many children they had, and how many times they moved, which does make it a little more interesting.

Stories without photos can be boring, though.

There, I said it.

Now, what if you were to *illustrate* the stories, and family trees, and vital records, and census forms by adding photos to them? And drawings? And maps? And local, regional, national, and global historical details, to put your ancestors' life experiences into perspective? And personal details gleaned from the census records, such as their occupations, where their parents were born, and whether they were educated?

Now it's getting interesting!

After all, if *you* don't preserve and share your family's photos, who will?

Are you ready to add photos to your family stories?

Let's get started! The next section will tell you how.

How to add photos to your stories

Here are some specific actions for you to take, depending on your desired goals. You don't have to do all the things! And you certainly don't have to do them all at once. You will enjoy the journey more if you take it a step at a time. Think of it as a new hobby, rather than a one-and-done event.

Low effort (*Do this if nothing else.*)

- Back up your photos! (*See: Are your files backed up?*)
- Store your photos in a clean, dry, cool place. Avoid steaming attics, dusty garages, and damp basements.

- Remove your photos from those old "magnetic" sticky albums. Photo organizers call these "chemical sandwiches", and they can do a lot of damage to your photos over time. If they are stuck in there, try loosening them with a piece of unwaxed dental floss. Or find more advice by searching online: *remove photos from sticky page albums.*

Medium effort *(Your family will thank you.)*

- Organize your photos so you can find the ones you want when you want them. *(See: Organize your photos)*

- Create a timeline of significant family events: births, marriages, deaths, moves, vacations, etc. Even if you don't organize all your photos yourself this will help someone else do it.

- Use acid-free, lignin-free storage boxes and supplies. You get extra credit if they pass the PAT (Photographic Activity Test). Not all "archival" products are what they are advertised to be, but Archival Methods and Native Archival are both industry partners of The Photo Managers. *(See: Knowledge, Inspiration & Assistance)*

- Go through your photos matching appropriate ones to the stories you wrote in Part 1. Think of them as illustrations.

- Pay attention when you find a photo that reminds you of a story you haven't told yet. Jot down a few notes to embellish upon later, so you don't forget.

- Print the best and most important of your digital photos on real photographic paper to share, enjoy, and preserve them. (It counts as a form of backup!)

- Digitally scan and store the best and most important of your printed photos. (300 dpi is the lowest recommended resolution; 600 dpi or higher is required if you ever want to enlarge the image.) File them apart from all the informational and trivial photos you take each day. And don't forget about the photos you have displayed in frames! Often those are the only copy we have, so scanning them is a must to secure a backup.

High effort (*Ask for help if you need it.*)

- Search for family photos that you never even knew existed. (*See: Where to find more photos*)

- If your photos need enhancement or repair, and you're not a Photoshop expert, try some of the digital tools offered by MyHeritage or Vivid-Pix.

- Create a SmugMug website for sharing digital photos with other family members. Or deposit them into an account such as Dropbox or FOREVER. My current favorite sharing tool is an app called Collectionaire. It does not store anything except a collection of links to wherever your photos, family trees, and stories are already stored in the cloud. So, if your mom is using Google Photos, and you are using FOREVER, and your uncle has some family stories he's written on Word files stored in Dropbox, or has published on his blog, that's OK. They can all stay where they are and still be shared on Collectionaire.

- Follow photo organizers who also blog about family history, such as Caroline Guntur and Andi Willis. *(See: Knowledge, Inspiration & Assistance)*

- Hire a photo manager to help you organize, preserve, and share your photos. If your photos need enhancement or repair, they can point you in the right direction, whether that's a photo restoration expert or a software solution. *(See: Knowledge, Inspiration & Assistance)*

PHOTO STORY:
Family Resemblances

Photo credits:

Left – original family photo in author's possession

Right – used with permission from Diane E. Michael

The Photo:

Two men who resemble one another

The Story:

The man on the left is my maternal grandfather, George D. Hankins (1898-1974), whom I knew as a child. During my genealogy research, I determined that George's great-grandfather (and my 3rd-great-grandfather), was Jacob J. Kisling (1789-1855). I knew about him long before I ever discovered the photo on the right, posted by several distant cousins on Ancestry.com. Note the similarities in face, build, pose, hands (clenched), and hair. Just because two people look alike doesn't mean they're related, of course, and biological family members can look quite different from one another. But if you have already established the relationship with research, a look-alike ancestor photo can feel like confirmation that you were on the right track.

(A longer version of this story, with more photos, appears in my guest blog post on thephotoorganizers.com: *Who Do You Think You Look Like? The Mystery of Family Resemblances.)*

Organize your photos

Why organize your photos? We organize them for the same reason we organize anything else — so we can find what we want when we want it!

If we have thousands of disorganized digital photos spread across various electronic devices, it becomes frustrating to sort through them every time we want to look at a particular photo or show it to someone else. It's like a print photo becoming lost in a pile of paper clutter.

Photo organizers use a lot of technical terms — *referenced files*, *native file structure*, *metadata*, *acid-free*, and *archival quality*. They use tools such as PhotoSweeper (for Mac) and Duplicate Cleaner Pro (for PC) for decluttering, and Photo Mechanic and Lightroom for editing and organizing digital photos. They create slideshows and photo books with tools that may or may not be around forever. They even use services that are, in fact, designed specifically to be around forever (such as FOREVER and Permanent)! Bold claims, but also, who am I to say they haven't got it all figured out? Time will tell!

You can use all these terms and tools too, of course, but whether you organize your own photos, or hire a pro to help you, it all starts here:

Do you know where your precious memories are?

Are they on your cell phone? And do you know how to get them *out* of your cell phone? Are they backed up in case something bad happens to your cell phone? *(See: Are your files backed up?)*

Are your digital photos spread across multiple directories, hard drives, and devices? Are your print photos languishing in dusty boxes in the garage or attic, or tucked under the bed? *(See: Where to find more photos)*

How to organize your photos

First, ask yourself, "Why am I doing this?" Knowing your "why" will make the rest of the project easier.

(See: 5 questions to ask yourself before organizing your memorabilia)

Next, start organizing. I've seen umpteen multi-step photo organizing processes. They all work, but I've never found an organizing situation yet that I couldn't adapt to Julie Morgenstern's SPACE formula: Sort, Purge, Assign, Containerize, Equalize (from her book, *Organizing From the Inside Out*).

Sort (group similar items)

- Gather all your photos together, from wherever they are. Pile print photos (and other analog formats such as slides and movie reels) into a box, or onto a table. For bringing digital images together from various sources you may need extra storage capacity in the form of an EHD (external hard drive). *(See: Where to find more photos)*

- Sort them into categories. For this we can use the ABCS of photo organizing (a term coined by Cathi Nelson, author of *Photo Organizing Made Easy,* and founder of The Photo Managers) as a guide:

- o A is for Album = These are your most album-worthy photos.
- o B is for Box = These photos aren't as great, but they're still keepers.
- o C is for Can = It's OK to "can" these. Seriously. Toss the "C" print photos into the trash can, and delete all the duplicate, blurry, and boring digital photos from your phone, camera, or computer.
- o S is for Story = These might not be the best quality photos, but if they help tell a story, keep them! And then don't forget to tell the story.

- Further categorize the photos you are keeping by person, date, location, or event. These categories are typical, but there are no right or wrong categories. You can even choose themes such as cars or houses your family has owned over the years and tell a story about them. Many photos will belong in more than one category, so you may want to keep track of that manually or digitally.

Purge (discard the excess)

- See "C is for Can" above. Keep in mind that most traditional printed photos are not recyclable due to their chemical coatings.

- Do you have print duplicates? Why not give them to relatives or friends who appear in the photos?

- Is there someone else, like a genealogical society, historical archive, university, social or civic organization, or professional association who might appreciate the photos you don't want? Ask them.

Assign (give things a home)

- Store print photos (and all forms of memorabilia) in a clean, dry, climate-controlled space. What room in your home would be suitable? Do you need to add shelving?

- Decide where you want to store your digital photos — on your computer? on an external hard drive? in cloud storage?

Containerize (use containers to group items)

- Photo-safe albums and boxes make great containers for print photos.

- Digital photos are contained in digital folders and files.

Equalize (maintain your system)

- Maintain the equilibrium of your system by frequently deleting poor (by your standards), utilitarian, duplicate, and unimportant photos.

- Place new photos in their assigned homes so you can find them later.

- Back up your photos! *(See: Are your files backed up?)*

- Use your organized system to find photos to display, share, enjoy, identify, and tell stories about!

Once your photos are organized, it will be much easier to be creative and meet your other photo goals.

Are your files backed up?

The last thing you want, after all your hard work, is to lose your files! So, you'll want to make sure they're backed up.

What does "backed up" mean, exactly?

"Backing up" your files is not just making a copy. It means making multiple copies of the original files and storing them in different places. This way, if one copy (or the original) is damaged or destroyed, you will still have one or more backup copies in another format and/or in another location. Things happen — to computers, cameras, phones, external hard drives (EHDs), thumb drives, backup services, cloud storage companies, etc. So *when* — not *if* — something happens, you will be glad you backed up your files.

Which files should you back up?
Back up anything you have created yourself or curated from the internet, including documents, digital photos, videos, presentations, family trees, etc. Programs and software are relatively available and easy to reinstall, but your personal files are a one-of-a-kind collection. Back them up!

There are services available to help you do this automatically. I used Carbonite for many years (with my PC), and currently use Backblaze and Time Machine (with my Mac). I have heard complaints that Carbonite takes too long for the initial back up, or too long to restore files when transferring them from an old computer to a new one. That's usually because the user has selected for back up, and is trying to restore, programs and software (which are easily re-installed) in addition to the personal files they've created or curated. Conversely, if you are using Backblaze and are not aware that it *will not* back up your operating system and applications (because they don't want to waste your bandwidth or their datacenter disk space), you could be in for a surprise.

Don't put all your eggs in one basket

Follow the "3-2-1 Rule", a computer industry best practice for backup and recovery:

- Keep at least 3 copies of your data, including the original.

- Keep the backed-up data on 2 different storage types to minimize the risk of one type of storage failure.

- Keep at least 1 copy of the data offsite. The cloud counts as an offsite location, as does a hard drive at your office, a friend's house, or a safety deposit box.

Digital Photo Backup

Storage options for copies of your digital photos include internal hard drives (your original files on your computer count as a copy), external or removable hard drives (including thumb drives), and cloud storage.

In addition to originals on my phone and computer, I use Dropbox cloud storage, and an external hard drive

(EHD). My iPhone syncs with my Mac through iCloud, and when I had an Android, I chose settings that sent copies of my photos through cyberspace directly to Dropbox. This way, I'm not worried about losing all my photos if my phone is stolen or gets dropped into a mud puddle. If you don't trust "the cloud," at the very least hook your phone up to your computer once a week and download the photos to your hard drive!

Another form of backing up digital photos is to print some of them onto photo paper. (Not regular, multipurpose printer paper.) Make photo books as gifts for your family. Frame a few to display and enjoy.

Passwords

One of my most important "documents" to back up is the contents of my digital password manager, LastPass. I periodically export a copy of all my passwords and save them as a file on my computer. I label the file something other than "passwords" and make sure a trusted friend, family member, or neighbor knows how to find it. I would only need the file if something happened to technically prevent my being able to access Last Pass. And my trusted person would only need the file if they were called upon to act on my behalf while I'm traveling or incapacitated.

Backing up is not just for computers

Don't forget to back up paper too! What do I mean by that? Well, consider your most important paper documents, scrapbooks, and photo albums. How would they fare in a flood or fire? Do they need to be digitized for safekeeping?

You probably have way too many papers and photos to want to scan them all. You might not even have a scanner. Start with the most important 20% of your paper items. If you can't choose, a professional organizer can guide you. And a photo organizer can help you scan. Some organizers can do both. *(See: Knowledge, Inspiration & Assistance)*

Don't do these things!

Finally, if you are sending all your photos directly to Facebook, *and if that is your only copy of them*, STOP IT RIGHT NOW! That's even worse than putting all your eggs in one basket because they only store *compressed* versions of your photos there. They are fine for internet sharing, but you will be disappointed if you ever want to make full-sized, enlarged, printed copies of them.

Similarly, I know family historians who have all their genealogy records on Ancestry.com, or another site. Those records also need to be saved in a genealogy program that lives on your computer and/or filed and backed up some other way. I use Family Tree Maker and others swear by Roots Magic. Both sync with Ancestry.com for easy back-ups.

What about you? Are *your* files backed up?
Remind your friends, too. Remember: Friends don't let friends put all their eggs in one basket!

Where to find more photos

Before you worry about not having enough photos, or where to find more, think about all the places where you've already stashed photos and other visual media. Gather them all together. Or at least make an inventory list. *(See: Organize your photos)*

Digital photos

- Computer hard drives
- External hard drives
- Thumb drives
- Smartphones
- Email and text attachments
- Memory cards in old cameras and desk drawers
- Cloud storage

Analog photos

- Albums
- Boxes stashed in a closet or under a bed
- Boxes stored in the garage, basement, or attic
- Slide carousels
- Film in canisters and cameras
- Negatives
- Movie film reels
- Video tapes

Then search for photos you don't already have in your possession.

- Ask your immediate and extended family what photos they have, and whether they are willing to share. Break the ice by sharing a photo with them that you think they may like or ask questions about one that intrigues you. While you're at it, why not compare versions of the family stories you've heard? Family history is a great excuse to connect with relatives!

- Connect with distant cousins. It doesn't matter where they live — even abroad! — or how far they are from you on your family tree. I call them "genealogy cousins" (strangers who are researching the same lines, or collateral families, or whose DNA matches yours) and I meet them on sites like Ancestry.com and FamilySearch. If they have posted photos of your mutual ancestors, there may be more where those came from!

- Search online, including Google Images, for the name and location of your ancestor. If there's something unique about them, like the name of a family business, search for that too.

- Google Maps (with its various satellite and street views) is a great resource for seeing what a location looks like today. Maybe your ancestors' home is still standing, and you can get a screenshot of it. Or go visit! Try to find cemeteries, schools, and other locations that are meaningful to your family.

- Check Newspapers.com (paid subscription site) or Chronicling America (free website). Many old newspaper photos I've found are of very poor quality. But some of them are good, or better than nothing. Once you know a photo exists, you may find someone else who has a better copy.

- Join special interest social media groups researching the same surnames, locations, religions, societies, and time frames as you.

- Both genealogy websites and brick-and-mortar historical society and genealogy libraries contain county histories, yearbooks, vertical files, and other records that may contain photos of your ancestors.

- Long shot: Check the Dead Fred "orphan photo" website to see if anyone's posted a photo pertaining to your family.

Now that we've told a few stories, and illustrated them with some of our organized photos, let's see what else is possible.

Part 3:
Dig Deeper & Climb Higher

*You live as long as
you are remembered.*

—*Russian proverb*

Why genealogy?

So far, we've talked about how to find stories to enhance your photos, and vice versa. Digging deeper means learning more about your family by doing a little research. If you already have a pedigree chart, this means adding more roots and branches. Or, perhaps filling in a few more leaves. Family tree roots grow deep, and branches grow high, so, let's dig deeper and climb higher!

What? You're not a genealogist? That's OK, I wasn't either... until I got bit by the genealogy bug.

How I got hooked on genealogy

My extended family was small, but far-flung. We didn't talk much about family history at home. One day, my dad gave me a small packet of genealogy materials which had been gathered by his uncle, whom I never knew. It covered my paternal great-grandparents and their descendants. It never even occurred to me to try to find out more until I was an adult and a good friend showed me how to research my family tree.

My first real independent discovery (something that wasn't mentioned in the packet, and not anything my dad had ever heard before), is that we are descended from a long line of Quakers. So long a line that my ancestors may have personally known George Fox, founder of the Quaker movement, in 1652 England. (This fact has yet to be proven, but that's where the research trail is leading me.)

Once I discovered the Charity Cook book, the subject of my next Photo Story — and not at all what it sounds like — I was hooked!

Eventually the Thornton family (our branch, at least) fell away from Quakerism, mostly due to marrying non-Quakers and being disowned for it. Surely my great-grandfather was either a Quaker too, or knew his father had been one? But within another generation the knowledge was lost. Until I found it.

What about you?

- Do you have knowledge that could be lost if you don't leave a record of it?

- Is there a photo of an ancestor that makes you curious to know more about them?

- Would you like to get to the bottom of a sketchy family story you've heard? Or a believable story that you'd like to document? Be prepared for it to not be true in quite the way you always heard it! *(See: PHOTO STORY: The Gangster Hideout)*

- Is there a time or place in your ancestors' lives that you'd like to know more about?

Are you ready to dig deeper and climb higher?

Let's get started! The next section will tell you how.

How to get started with genealogy

Here are some specific actions for you to take, depending on your desired goals. You don't have to do all the things! And you certainly don't have to do them all at once. You will enjoy the journey more if you take it a step at a time. Think of it as a new hobby, rather than a one-and-done event.

Low effort *(Do this if nothing else.)*

- Decide if conducting genealogy research is for you. *(See: Puzzling Out Your Family History)*
- Then, whether or not you will be doing your own research, determine your genealogy goals. *(See: Climbing your never-ending family tree)*

- Download *family group sheets* from the internet (or from my Org4life.com website). Make several copies and fill them out as best you can. List yourself on the first sheet as a child, along with your biological (or adoptive) parents and siblings. Then fill one out for your mother as a child with her family. And one for your father as a child with his family. Then a sheet for each of their parents. And so on. Work backward in time, one step at a time. Don't skip any steps! Don't worry about what you don't know. Just fill in what you do know.

- Ask family members (if available) for additional information to fill in the family group sheets so that these details are not lost to time.

Medium effort (*Your family will thank you.*)

- Interview relatives. If "interview" sounds too fancy or difficult, just ask them questions and take notes, or record their answers to preserve their voices:
    - What was their life like?
    - How big was their family?
    - Where did they live?
    - Who were their neighbors?

- o How did they earn a living?
- o Why did they move (if they did)?
- o What historical events impacted them?
- o For many more ideas, search online: *family history questions*.
- o TIP: Show them a few photos to get them talking!

- Ask your relatives about family stories, rumors, and legends that you have heard. The truth may lie somewhere in the middle of the various versions of the story. (Be aware that they may be reluctant to talk about certain events or situations from the past. Don't press them if it will damage your relationship.)

- Use history books, maps, and the internet to find out more about a particular time, place, or event. Add local, regional, and global historical details to put your family's stories into perspective.

- Organize your "family history" (an umbrella term which includes keepsakes, memorabilia, photos, genealogy research materials, medical history, and pedigree charts). Just do as much as you can. (*See: Organize your family history*)

High effort *(Ask for help if you need it.)*

- Reassure yourself that this endeavor is worthwhile. *(See: What if nobody else cares?)*

- Get your DNA tested. It's not difficult, and it has become more affordable, but it does take some effort to link the results to an online family tree and follow through when you are notified of matches. Be prepared for surprises and be sensitive to the feelings of others who may not want to be involved in your discoveries.

- Learn to do genealogy research online or in libraries. There are lots of free resources available to help you these days, including Crista Cowan's YouTube tutorials. *(See: Genealogy research at any budget. Also: Knowledge, Inspiration & Assistance)*

- Follow experts who write and post about genealogy in a way that demystifies the process and makes it seem doable and fun, like Lisa Lisson, Thomas MacEntee, Amy Johnson Crow, and Janine Adams. *(See Knowledge, Inspiration & Assistance)*

- Hit a brick wall in your research? We all do, from time to time. Don't give up, though! Just take a break from that line of inquiry and come back later with some fresh new ideas. Work on something else meanwhile. You can also get empathy and support from others in the same boat in online genealogy forums. *(See: 20 reasons why you can't find your ancestor)*

- Hire a genealogist to research your family tree for you. *(See Knowledge, Inspiration & Assistance)*

PHOTO STORY:
The Charity Cook Book

Photo Credit:
Hazel Thornton

The Photo:

Book Cover: *Charity Cook: A Liberated Woman*, by Algie I. Newlin, Illustrated by S. Combs (Friends United Press, 1981)

The Story:

My 5th-great-grandmother, Charity Wright Cook (1745-1822), was a Quaker minister who traveled frequently — including overseas — while her husband, Isaac Cook (1743-1820), stayed home and took care of their 11 children. (Well, I'm sure the older children took a great deal of the care of the younger ones.) Her granddaughter, Charity Cook Thornton, and husband Nathan Thornton were the first new couple I "discovered" as a genealogist. According to a Polk County, Iowa county history, their son Calvin was "reared as a Quaker." Prior to that, my family had no inkling that we were descended from a long line of Quakers!

(A longer version of this story appears in my Org4life.com blog post: *Thornton Family History Lost and Found*)

Genealogy is for everybody!

What comes to mind when you hear the word *genealogy*? Does it sound boring and time-consuming? Or does it sound fascinating in the same way that solving a mystery or reading historical fiction can be?

Pedigree charts might sound fancy, but they're really just ancestor charts, or written-down family trees. And everybody has a family tree! If you think pedigrees are just for royalty, dogs, and horses, think again!

Top 10 reasons why genealogy might be for you:

1. Genealogy is fascinating and fun! Do you like puzzles? Mysteries? History? Family? No wonder it's such an increasingly popular hobby!

2. It can bring your family closer together. Share your research (and photos and stories) with your family. Interview your elders before it's too late. Teach your children about history in a way that feels personal and relevant to them.

3. Genealogy can be part of organizing for your legacy (Part 4), especially if you are the keeper of the family's history.

4. It combines well with other hobbies and interests, such as reading, writing, travel, photography, geography, history, sociology, scrapbooking, fashion, cooking, etc.

5. It will probably inspire you to organize your photos and keepsakes, as well as your vital documents (birth, marriage, and death certificates) and other important items. *(See: Organize your family history. Also: Organize your photos)*

6. It's free! Or, at least, it can be. Genealogy is available to anyone at any budget, including lots of free online resources. Try Family Search, Google (or the search engine of your choice), and Cyndi's List for starters. Also, don't forget free brick-and-mortar libraries, including LDS Family History Centers, which are open to the public. *(See: Genealogy research at any budget)*

7. You can put your own twist on it. Did you know there are people who specialize in researching specific regions, ethnic groups, or religions? Some researchers focus on one-name studies (e.g., all Thorntons, directly related or not), or they specialize in military history, adoption, or property records. (You could call yourself a House Detective!) Such specialties can apply to professionals and amateurs alike. Speaking of which…

8. Does "genealogist" sound too scholarly, or intimidating to you…? You can call yourself whatever you like: Genealogist, Researcher, Family Historian, Ancestry Detective, Bloodline Sleuth, Storyteller, Family Tree Climber, Seeker of Dead Relatives, etc. Whatever you call yourself, is OK.

9. You can do it yourself. Or DIY with a little help. Even if you are already the family historian, or photo keeper, you might need some support in organizing your photos and records. *(See: Knowledge, Inspiration & Assistance)*

10. You can hire someone to do it for you. A pedigree chart, in a family history binder full of supporting documents and photos, makes a great gift for yourself, or for a loved one! *(See: Knowledge, Inspiration & Assistance)*

Are you curious about your roots? Do you have a family mystery to solve? The next section — *Puzzling Out Your Family History* — will help you figure out if genealogy research is for you.

Puzzling out your family history

Is genealogy research for you? I like to compare genealogy research to working a jigsaw puzzle. Sound fun? It is!

It can also be challenging. Imagine that there are dozens of puzzles, all mixed together (one for each nuclear family), and many of the puzzle pieces are broken or missing, and there are extra pieces thrown in there from other people's puzzles, and you don't have any of the boxes with the pictures on them to guide you. Sound tough? It can be, and yet, it is so rewarding when the pieces start to fit together, and the picture starts to take shape!

Here are some things to consider, and ways in which you will need to get organized, if you want to puzzle out your own family history:

Your Goals

Is there a family mystery you'd like to solve? Or a family legend you'd like to prove (or disprove)?

It's important to know what you want so you can focus your efforts. Do you want to share your research with loved ones? Are you looking to create a family tree? A book of stories about your ancestors? A photo collage? Are you interested in collaborating with others? Do you want to *go wide* — stopping with your 8 great-grandparents (or 16 great-great-grandparents)? Or do you want to *go deep* — tracing a particular line back across the centuries and continents? *(See: Climbing your never-ending family tree)*

Your Workspace

Do you have a table or desk that is either dedicated, or can be easily cleared, to make enough workspace for your project? Are your records and notes paper or electronic? Do you have some of both?

Your Stuff

What about your photos and your records? Are they organized? There is no right or wrong way to organize your materials, but if it's not organized, and kept handy, you won't be able to find what you need to help you work effectively. You don't want to have to dig it out of a box in the closet each time you want to work! *(See: Organize your family history. Also: Organize your photos)*

Your Time

Genealogy is a project that cannot be completed overnight. Let me rephrase that: Genealogy is a project that cannot be completed. At all. Ever. The more you learn about your family, the more you realize there is to learn. The more ancestors you discover, the more there are to discover. All of your ancestors have ancestors too! So, just accept right now that you are going to do a little at a time. Schedule regular time to pursue your goals. Don't wait until you "find" time! *(See: Climbing your never-ending family tree)*

Your Tools and Resources

I started out as an old-school pre-internet genealogist, when my only choices were to drive to local LDS Family

History Centers, genealogical societies, and libraries to examine county histories, maps, and microfilm records.

When I had enough information to make the trip worthwhile, I'd travel, armed with my pedigree chart and family group sheets, to the locations where my ancestors lived. I'd visit small-town city halls (the kind with dusty basements full of seldom-used record ledgers) and old cemeteries (some of which are in current-day cow pastures, or behind private residences). I still highly recommend on-location field trips, but my goodness, it's amazing what's available online these days!

Ancestry.com is an invaluable resource (although certainly not the only one). Census records! DNA testing! Quaker meeting records! Military records! Links to other family trees! Oh my! But please, I implore you to not merge your tree with someone else's just because you've found one of your ancestors on it. You don't know where that information came from, or how accurate it is. (Although, I must say, the internet is making it easier and easier to find out.) The other person may have copied someone, who copied someone else (just like you are tempted to do), who had no idea what they were doing.

Your Family

Start with what (and whom) you know first-hand (your parents and siblings) and work methodically back through time. Don't skip steps. Find out who else in your family is doing research (or has possession of family records and photos) and compare notes. If you don't know any relatives who are interested, or who can give you a jump-start, you may find some distant cousins online who are researching the same branches.

Learn about DNA tests and figure out who would be the best person(s) to take one to help further your research. Several members of my family have already been tested. At first, I was disappointed in the results, because they were so vague. If you and I are a "match," I really don't care if our ancestors were all Vikings 1000 years ago. What I want to know is who Thomas Thornton's parents were (1698 – 1762 Virginia), and where his ancestors lived before coming to America. (England? But where, specifically? I want to visit!)

The more people got tested, though, the larger the database grew and the more refined the results became. In the years since I took the test, there are several new tools for analyzing matches, and I've now been linked by DNA to others who are also researching "my" Thomas Thornton.

Your Mind

Do you have the curiosity, determination, and mental stamina to do research? A healthy skepticism, and ability to accept the truth, whatever it turns out to be? Do you enjoy a good mystery? Working puzzles? Playing detective? Then you'll make a great family genealogist!

If I have sparked an interest in doing your own genealogy research, great. If not, though, that's OK. But please keep reading. The next section is for you even if you haven't caught the genealogy bug, and even if you don't think you ever will.

Organize your family history

Maybe you've decided genealogy research isn't for you. Why, then, should you still organize your family history?

Because family history is not just about doing research. It's about making historical items and information accessible to your family and generations to come.

Sometimes when I talk about *family history* I am, indeed, referring to genealogy research. But not always. So, what else falls under the umbrella term *family history*? Think about your own items as you read this list. Some of them will fall into more than one category.

Family history includes:

- **Keepsakes:** Items kept in memory of whoever gave or originally owned them.

- **Memorabilia:** Objects kept or collected because of their historical interest, especially those associated with memorable people or events.

- **Photos**: If we collect nothing else, consider this: we all take more photos every day with our digital phone cameras than our ancestors took in their entire lifetimes!

- **Genealogy research materials:** These range from vital records (birth, marriage, and death certificates) and census records to research notes, historical and biographical documents and books, maps, photos (paper and digital), and family bibles.

- **Medical history:** This can be important to know when faced with the possibility or actuality of certain illnesses and conditions.

- **Pedigree chart:** AKA family tree, this is the most common way to organize the information gleaned from genealogy research materials.

Why organize it all?

- So that you can easily find what you are looking for when you want to read it, use it, admire it, display it, share it with others, update it, or reminisce.

- To be prepared in the case of illness (medical history) or death (think: obituary, tribute slide show, etc.).

- To be prepared in the case of a natural disaster (think: backing up your files and grab-and-go bags).

- So that someone else (in the event you are no longer available) can make sense of your memorabilia and research. Don't let your treasures and hard work go to waste!

- So that your space, your mind, and your computer hard drive don't get cluttered with so many things that the important papers, files, and keepsakes get lost in the shuffle.

- So that you don't miss valuable genealogy clues, or puzzle pieces, hidden in your mystery piles of paper.

- So that your work area isn't a mess that distracts you from being productive and enjoying your genealogy research or your photo and storytelling projects.

When is the best time to organize your family history? As you can probably guess, the best time is NOW. But there are some other good times, such as:

- The New Year. Why? Because getting organized is always one of the top 5 resolutions.
- When a child or grandchild is born, graduates, or gets married.
- When a parent reaches a milestone birthday or retirement.
- When someone — you, or a loved one — falls ill or dies, but hopefully long before that happens, so you're prepared.

Which of your family history categories have you already organized? Which ones need some work?

PHOTO STORY: Skeletons in the Family Closet

Photo Credit: Department of Corrections
San Quentin Prisoner Photograph [Franklin W. Thornton, #18352]
California State Archives, Office of the Secretary of State

The Photo:

Old-fashioned prisoner mug shots

The Story:

I found this photo on Ancestry.com. The last three circled images are of Franklin Wilburforce Thornton (1856-1928). Note the identifying information written on the chalkboards in the bottom row of photos. Doesn't he look creepy in his mug shots? They all do. Maybe because they aren't smiling. And isn't it interesting how they photographed everyone with hat, without hat, and then completely shaved, in prison stripes?

Frank is my 3rd-great-half-uncle — so, not a direct ancestor, but who could resist trying to find out more?

A little Newspapers.com research told me he was a photographer who spent 3 years in San Quentin for embezzlement. Embezzlement of what? Postage stamps! Postage stamps? I kid you not. $762 worth. (That amount, in 1899, is equivalent to $25,183 today.)

There was even a nation-wide manhunt. They finally found him in Ohio, where he gave himself up. Everyone who knew him claimed to be shocked at his disappearance.

Upon further investigation, it was more that he worked in the post office and skimmed money from postage stamp sales than what I had imagined — loading himself up with arms full of postage stamps and fleeing with them. But still, now I'm wondering why he did it and what it was like when he finally returned to his family?

Genealogy research at any budget

Are you the family historian? Are you curious about your past?

Genealogy research can be an expensive hobby if you factor in computer programs, tools, memberships, documentation fees, research trips, books, seminars, and conferences! (Hmmm, now I wonder how much I've spent over the years? Not to mention the time invested…)

But it doesn't have to cost a penny.

Here are some options for researching and organizing your documents, memorabilia, and photos, in order of affordability.

Almost-free ways to do genealogy research:

- People have been using paper records and storing their pedigree charts in binders and folders for centuries. And they still work!

- Download *family group sheets* from the internet (or from my Org4life.com website). Make several copies and fill them out as best you can. *(See: How to get started with genealogy)*

- Interview your oldest relatives, and those in precarious health, before it's too late! Don't wait.

- Gather family documents, old bibles, certificates, records, and photographs, and store them somewhere safe (after you enter the relevant data on your family group sheets).

- There are lots of free online resources. Try Family Search, Google (or the search engine of your choice), Cyndi's List, and Crista Cowan's Ancestry YouTube tutorials for starters. *(See: Knowledge, Inspiration & Assistance)*

- Check your local public library to see if they offer free access to the library edition of Ancestry.com, Fold3 (military records), and other databases, as mine does.

- Visit other libraries in your area, including LDS Family History Centers, which are open to the public. The people who work there are usually very helpful.

- Use Evernote, OneNote, Apple Notes, or your own unique filing system, to organize your electronic records, digital photos, scans of print photos and records, and the information you find online. *(See: Organize your family history)*

- Check out my Org4life.com Genealogy Resource Roundup for more ideas. Check back often for updates! *(See: Org4life Resources)*

Inexpensive ways to do genealogy research:

- Join a local genealogy society, or one in a region you are researching. The annual fee is usually nominal, and some of them provide free public webinars throughout the year, with archived webinars available to members only. One of my favorites is the Southern California Genealogical Society, host of the annual Genealogy Jamboree.

- Purchase a genealogy program for your computer, such as Family Tree Maker or Roots Magic, to help you keep track of your data and share it with others. Don't forget to back up your computer files! *(See: Are your files backed up?)*

- Check out GenealogyBargains.com for, well, genealogy bargains of all kinds! *(See: Knowledge, Inspiration & Assistance)*

Worthwhile investments:

- Subscribe to one or more genealogy services such as Ancestry.com, MyHeritage, or Findmypast, at whatever level of membership works for you.

- Hire a professional genealogist to help you. *(See: Knowledge, Inspiration & Assistance)*

Strategies I DO NOT Recommend:

- Do nothing.
- Continue letting valuable documents and photos languish and deteriorate in boxes in the attic or garage.

- Procrastinate on asking the older generation about their lives — and who's in all those photos? — until it's too late.
- Delay organizing your own genealogy materials — unless, of course, you don't want to make your research easier and more effective!
- Risk leaving all your hard work to someone who won't be able to make heads or tails of it.

I hope this list has given you some ideas that sound affordable to you.

Next let's look at putting some boundaries around your never-ending genealogy project.

Climbing your never-ending family tree

Your family tree is never really finished! It is forever growing at both ends. Roots grow deep, and branches grow high. Your ancestors' descendants are continually being born (even if not to you, personally, or even to your branch of the family). No matter how many branches and leaves you've added in the past, there are always more for you to discover.

Just think, the number of your direct ancestors doubles with each generation. You have 2 parents, 4 grandparents, 8 great-grandparents, and so on. After only 6 generations there are a cumulative total of 126 direct ancestors, each of whose DNA eventually played a part in making YOU.

As a genealogist, it's important for me to be able to define my scope of work for a client project. And it's important for YOU, if you are the family historian, to keep your goals in mind, too. Define your genealogy projects, so you don't end up working endlessly and randomly.

Going Wide / Going Deep / Focusing

Everyone has a different motivation for taking a closer look at their family history. As a researcher, I like to tell clients I can *go wide*, I can *go deep*, or I can *focus*.

You might want to *go wide* if:

- You are starting from not knowing much and want to learn a little about all the main branches of your family.
- You want a nicely filled out 4-generation pedigree chart.

You might want to *go deep* if:

- You want to see how far back in time you can trace a particular branch of your family.

- You are curious about where a specific branch of your family came from.

- You want to know how a branch of your family fits into historical context.

- You want to learn more about a branch's migration patterns, naming patterns, or family business.

You might want to *focus* on one ancestor, or location, or time period if:

- One of them is noteworthy or mysterious.

- There is a family story you'd like to prove or disprove.

- You'd like to know more about the place, time, activities, and life of a specific ancestor.

Telling the story

Whether you *go wide, go deep,* or *focus* to begin with, you can always explore something else next time. Or maybe your next project will be to spend some time adding more personal and colorful details in the form of photos, stories, and historical context to the story. After all, that's what it's all about, isn't it? The stories?

Hit a brick wall?

*20 reasons why you
can't find your ancestor*

Can't find your ancestor? Getting frustrated? Ready to give up?

We all hit a seemingly-impenetrable "brick wall" in our genealogy research now and then, and it's easy to get discouraged. Don't give up, though! Take a break — five minutes or five years, I've done both — and return to your research with some fresh ideas!

Here are some of the possible reasons why you can't find your ancestor:

1. **The record doesn't exist.** Some records never existed to begin with, because not all record-keeping started at the same time in all locations. (The mystery of where my Grandma Hankins was born, for example, is too long a story to tell here, but it provided a great test case for my budding detective skills!) Other records were lost to time or natural disaster (like the 1890 U.S. census records, which were largely lost to fire). Or maybe you are looking among civil records, but your ancestor was a Quaker, and you really need to be looking at the Society of Friends' meeting minutes for a particular location and timeframe.

2. **The record exists, but it's not online yet.** There is still great value in visiting libraries, cemeteries, and other repositories of genealogical records! The one you need may be literally sitting on a dusty shelf in the basement of the city hall where your ancestor lived. (Ask me how I know.)

3. **The record is online, but it's not indexed yet.** Thus, it is not easily searched for and found. Volunteering on Family Search to help index records won't help you find *your* ancestor, but it

will help other people find theirs. So, it's good karma and it will give you an understanding of how indexing errors happen.

4. **You haven't yet recognized or accepted that the "wrong" surname spelling might, indeed, be your ancestor!** (There are many reasons why and how this happens. Maybe this is a chapter for my next book?)

5. **There's a typo (or other error) in the index,** transcript, abstract, database, written family history, or other derivative source. Check the original record if possible. (Vital records such as birth, death, and marriage certificates are considered primary sources; they can contain their own errors.)

6. **Illegible handwriting, and misinterpretation** of perfectly good old-fashioned script, causes errors at every level (this applies to original documents, transcription, and indexing).

7. **The record or index used initials only.** Ugh! I hate when that happens!

8. **Your ancestor truncated, Anglicized, or completely changed his name** — but not because they forced him to at Ellis Island, because that's a myth, albeit a popular one that I won't argue did *not* happen in *your* family. (Search online: *Ellis Island name change myth.*)

9. **Your ancestor went by a middle name, or a nickname**, and all you know is their first name, or vice versa, and they switched back and forth over time. Or, whoever reported or recorded the data did.

10. **It's an original record, but it's wrong.** Who supplied the information? Would they necessarily know? How close in time to the event — birth, marriage, death, etc. — was the record made?

11. **The census taker** interviewed whoever answered the door (whether or not they were the best person to ask); he wrote down what he heard (without concern for spelling); or he was tired or confused (or drunk!) and skipped that street altogether.

12. **The census says your ancestor was a different race than you expected** — so you're not sure if you've gotten off track — because the census taker reported whatever he thought, saw, or was told. (I have an ancestor who was reported as W [White], B [Black], and M [Mulatto] in different census years. She was a slave owner, too. Oh, the plot thickens!)

13. **People lived together in combinations you didn't expect.** (Who are these strangers with whom my great-grandfather is living as a child? Ohhh, I see now, his father died, and his mother remarried, that's all.)

14. **On the Ancestry.com search form, you have too much data in the search fields.** Delete some of it. Or, if you have too little info, add an educated guess (e.g., a good estimate for a parent's birth year is 20 years before the first known child's birth year) to see if it helps generate results.

15. **You are using your female ancestor's married name** to search for her birth certificate, or her maiden name to search for her death record. (In

Ancestry.com, if you have her in your tree by her married name, delete the surname so Ancestry.com doesn't think it's her maiden name. Better to leave it blank if you don't know her maiden name yet.)

16. **Your ancestor may have been married multiple times.** Which surname, or spouse, or children still living at home, would apply to the time frame you are seeking to know more about?

17. **Your ancestor may have moved.** I had family that I thought was moving house an awful lot. It turned out they didn't move at all, but the county lines kept changing around them from one census decade to the next.

18. **You are looking only for vital records** (birth, marriage, death). Try something different, like land records, wills, military pension files, and newspaper articles.

19. **You are focused only your direct ancestors.** Try broadening the search a little by researching their siblings too. Learn more about their FAN club

(Friends, Associates, and Neighbors, a well-known acronym coined by Elizabeth Shown Mills.)

20. **You have made an error** somewhere and are now off climbing someone else's tree. Oops! Taking it one leaf and branch at a time, carefully documenting each step, will help avoid that. Go back and check your work.

I hope something in this list will lead you to a brick wall breakthrough. Or, if nothing else, perhaps it will give you some insight into why you can't find what you're looking for and encourage you to keep looking!

So, why go to all this trouble if no one else cares about your research? Well, you wouldn't be alone if you felt that way. Keep reading…

What if nobody
else cares?

What if nobody else cares about your personal or family history? Did you know that not everyone cares about genealogy? I know, right? Gasp! I have found, when it comes to genealogy, that there are three types of people:

1. **Don't know; don't care.** Those who don't know much about their family history, and who don't really care, either. These people likely did not grow up with stories. Maybe the stories were lost. Maybe those who could have told the stories died, or were inhibited in some way by privacy, shyness, or shame. Family secrets can be very powerful things!

2. **"Our family tree is finished."** Ugh! First, it's never really finished! *(See: Climbing your never-ending family tree)* But also, I feel sorry for people in this category, because they may never know the pleasure of getting to know their ancestors or experience the satisfaction of discovering a new branch of their tree. Sometimes what has already been done is only a couple of branches wide, or a few generations deep. And sometimes it's slightly-to-highly inaccurate. I know that's disappointing, but have you tried to verify it yourself, branch by branch, and leaf by leaf?

3. **Rabid genealogists.** This label can be worn proudly no matter how much, or how little, actual research experience one has. There are people without trees because all they wanted from their DNA test was the ethnicity estimate report. And there are others who started trees and abandoned them because they didn't know what to do next, or they didn't have time to work on them. But I don't know anyone who has made an independent discovery — by locating and analyzing records — who didn't get hooked. The

thrill of the hunt and the satisfaction of fitting a puzzle piece into place is contagious! *(See: Puzzling out your family history)*

But…what if you're a rabid genealogist and your family is "Don't know, don't care"?

Or, what if you don't have any children, or other living family members, or anyone else who shares your interest, who can use, appreciate, and preserve your research when you are gone?

Don't despair!

If your family is not interested in your research, think about why that might be:

- Are they busy with their lives, and too tired to care about your hobby?
- Do they live far away, so it's difficult to share your excitement with them?
- Do you show them only boring names, dates, and places? Are they lacking the stories and the photos that would make them more interesting?

Here are some things you can do:

Embellish

Add stories! *(See: Part 1)* Add photos! *(See: Part 2)* Dig deeper and climb higher! *(See: Part 3)* If adding photos and stories to your pedigree charts does not magically make your family fall in love with your ancestors the way you have, or if there's seemingly no one to leave your research and your stories to, you'll need to think bigger.

Share

There are lots of ways to share your research — and your photos and stories — with your family. And most of them are problematic. You can create a family website, though that's easier said than done. Or put everything in cloud storage, such as Dropbox, that everyone can access, but which requires them to open individual files to see what's inside. It can be equally challenging to get family members to share *their* photos and stories with *you*! My current favorite sharing tool is an app called Collectionaire. *(See: How to add photos to your stories)*

Keep in mind, as you'll read more about in Part 5, that apps and platforms are constantly changing and leapfrogging one another. But they also tend to improve over time!

Document

The more organized your genealogy materials are, both physically and digitally, and the more well-documented your findings, the more sense someone else will be able to make of them in the event you are not there to explain it all to them. *(See: Organize your family history)*

Donate

You may find that a genealogical society or library, or a historical archive, is interested in your research. It could be an institution that is local to you, or one that is specific to a region or topic you have researched. Be sure to ask them first, though, before dumping it on them, and do them the favor of organizing your materials before donating them.

Upload

Upload your well-researched tree and supporting documentation, stories, and photos to websites such as Ancestry.com and FamilySearch.org for others who are more distantly related to find and enjoy. Future generations that you will never meet will thank you for it!

Bottom line

It's OK if you don't have children or other heirs to carry on the genealogy torch for you. Remember: Your *ancestors* have *many descendants*, on *many branches* of the family tree besides yours. The further back you go, the more ancestors (with descendants) there are. And, on some of those other branches, there are descendants who would love to compare their notes with yours! It might be your nephew who becomes the next family historian. Or it might be your 3rd-cousin-twice-removed, whom you've never met, and her descendants, who will benefit from your research.

I promise that, with a little effort, your hard work won't go to waste!

PHOTO STORY:
The Gangster Hideout

Photo Credit:
Archie R. Thornton Jr.

The Photo:

A big white house with pillars in front

The Story:

This is the home where my mom was born and lived as a child. At that time, the red brick had not yet been painted white, and the stately pillars had not yet been added by a subsequent owner. It is located by the Mississinewa River in Eaton, Indiana (near Muncie), at the end of an otherwise deserted dirt road. That's me on the porch with my mom and brother during a visit. As the story goes, my grandparents bought this house "for dirt cheap" because no one else wanted to live there. (They didn't use the second story during the winter because they couldn't afford to heat it.) That's because, at one time, it had been a gangster hideout. We couldn't remember who, though, and thought it might have been John Dillinger. Was it Dillinger? Was the story even true?

Some research on Wikipedia, Google Maps, and Newspapers.com confirmed that this house, indeed, had been a gangster hideout for a time. Eventually, Gerald Chapman (not John Dillinger) and his gang murdered the former homeowners — Yikes! — but at least they were out on the main road, in their car, and not actually inside the house at the time. I found them — the homeowners, not the gang — buried in the cemetery next door to the house. And part of the mystery has yet to be solved. If the gang, as rumored, left hidden treasure, will it ever be found? (My mom and her sisters searched, but with no luck.)

(A longer version of this story appears in my Org4life.com blog post: *Mom's Boxes Part 8: The Gangster Hideout*)

Part 4:
Leave a Legacy, Not a Burden

*I often ask myself,
will anyone I know
be happier if I save this?*

— *Margareta Magnusson,*
The Gentle Art of Swedish Death Cleaning:
How to Free Yourself and Your Family from a Lifetime of Clutter

Why leave a legacy?

Everyone leaves a legacy. You may think you have no legacy, but really, you have no choice but to leave one. The only question is: How much of a blessing or a burden will it be?

What is a legacy?

A legacy is anything you leave behind when you die. It can be a gift of money or property bequeathed to a person or an institution in a will. It can be a body of wisdom captured in a published book, or the ongoing good deeds of a non-profit organization that you founded or support. Or it could simply be the wonderful warm memories of you that live on in the hearts of friends and family after you're gone.

A legacy can also be the consequences of neglect. It could be a house full of clutter that no one knows how to manage. Or the lack of a will and a designated executor, leading to confusion and more money and time being spent on your estate than it's worth.

And if you don't think you have an "estate," think again.

What is an estate?

Your estate consists of both tangible and intangible possessions:

- **Tangible possessions** are your home, your car, everyday items, and keepsakes. (Do you have a will? Or, as some call it, a love letter to your family?)

- **Intangible possessions** are online bank accounts, social media and email accounts, website content, music and photo depositories, and other digital assets. (Do you also have a *virtual* will?)

Talking about death won't kill you, LOL!

This legacy stuff might sound morbid to some, but really, it's just a natural extension of my years working as a professional organizer. Clients tell me, "I don't want to leave a mess for my kids." And I say, "Great! Time to declutter, downsize, simplify, and organize."

Clearing physical and mental clutter gives you the freedom to live the life you really want. It also gives you the freedom of knowing you are not leaving a mess for your loved ones to clean up.

Preparing for the inevitable is just a way of clearing mental clutter. If there's one thing you *can't* count on, it's that nothing bad will ever happen. But don't worry; instead, take action!

Why not downsize now?

Most people think of downsizing in relation to moving from a large house to a smaller one. But clearing away possessions that you don't need or want can also be part of your legacy. It's never too early (or too late) to start downsizing, identifying your treasures, and telling their stories. *(See: Tell the stories of your things, too!)*

The alternative is that you leave so much stuff behind for your loved ones to go through and deal with that they will be overwhelmed. If they don't have clear instructions, they are likely to lump everything together and sell or donate it. Or, even worse, they will absorb your *entire household* of furniture and belongings into their own home simply because they feel guilty getting rid of it, or because they don't know what else to do with it.

Why not downsize and declutter now so your family doesn't have to do it for you when you're gone? Create peace of mind, for yourself and for your family, by making decisions now so they don't have to do it later.

As a genealogist, I hope you keep and share everything of positive emotional value and historical significance. And, as an organizer, I hope that focusing on the story-worthy possessions in your life will help you realize how much of the other stuff you don't really need.

Are you ready to leave *your* legacy?

Let's get started! The next section will tell you how.

How to leave a legacy

Here are some specific actions for you to take, depending on your desired goals. You don't have to do all the things! And you certainly don't have to do them all at once. You will enjoy the journey more if you take it a step at a time. Think of it as a new hobby, rather than a one-and-done event.

Low effort *(Do this if nothing else.)*

- Slap a super-sticky Post-it® note on the back, inside, or bottom of your valuable or sentimental items with the name of the person you want to leave it to, if you know. Add a reason why, or a little story about the item. (Keep in mind that even these super-sticky ones don't stick forever. This is best used as a temporary measure.)

- Tell your loved ones (verbally or in writing) the stories of your special belongings, so they can be distinguished from your not-so-special things.

- For inspiration, read *The Gentle Art of Swedish Death Cleaning,* by Margareta Magnusson. I promise this little book is a helpful and humorous read, not weighty, morbid, or depressing!

Medium effort *(Your family will thank you.)*

- Start decluttering, downsizing, simplifying, and organizing your home. It doesn't have to be a big overwhelming project. If you do a little at a time on a regular basis, it will become a habit which will pay off over time.

- Write stories, as long or as short as you like, and include new photos of the items you are writing about. Bonus points if you can match them up with old family photos. Do you have any photos showing the items being used, worn, or displayed? *(See: Tell the stories of your things, too!)*

- If feasible, attach numbers to the items and use the same numbers to identify the corresponding stories and photos, to create a little indexing system. If the items are too small, or there are many of them, store them in numbered containers.

- For items you're ready to part with, but want to remember; take photos of them, tell their stories, and then donate, sell, or give them away.

- For the items you've decided to keep, organize, store, preserve, use, honor, and share them.

- Create a personal inventory spreadsheet. Mine lists only the important items in my home. It designates who I want to inherit them (also giving them permission to not keep them forever) and includes strict instructions to sell or donate the rest to proactively alleviate any potential sense of guilt. Tell someone you trust that the document exists, what the filename is, and your computer password. Or leave instructions in an app such as LastPass or Everplans.

- Communicate with your adult children about the things you are saving to pass down to them. Be prepared in case they aren't interested. *(See: Sorry, your kids don't want your stuff)*

High effort (*Ask for help if you need it.*)

- Take photos of your valuables, and other important items, and document their provenance (their origin and how you came to have them), value (get appraisals where feasible), and stories in FairSplit, which is designed for helping families divide estates. Or save it all in an asset inventory app such as HomeZada or Pinventory.

- If you want to leave an item to someone, write it down or put it in your will so that your family is aware of your intentions.

- Organize your memorabilia. Decide what you want done with your photos, and other keepsakes. (*See: 5 questions to ask yourself before organizing your memorabilia*)

- Hire a professional organizer to help you get it done more quickly and easily. NAPO specialties include photography/memorabilia/collections, home inventories, estate management, digital organizing, downsizing, and more. (*See: Knowledge, Inspiration & Assistance*)

Tell the stories of your things, too!

When I help an organizing client sort through their deceased parent's belongings, the categories that emerge are usually: *Keep, Share with Family, Toss, Donate,* and *Whaaaat?* While that last category can be good for some laughs, it can also be overwhelming to those who are grieving a loss.

Not everything is story-worthy
Much of our stuff is just everyday stuff! And if no one knows what else to do with it, the treasures get packed up (or disposed of) along with the junk.

Sometimes the boxes we are sorting through have been sitting in the garage for years. The client wants my organizing assistance, but they also want my comforting presence. They fear it will be too painful to open the boxes alone because of the memories with which they will surely be flooded. Indeed, sometimes there are tears, but as often as not they are from laughing (with relief) at what we find:

- Dishtowels, still in the package, that were never used and do not seem special in any way.
- Clothing that the client does not recognize.
- Books that the previous owner may have read and enjoyed, but which also may have just been sitting on their shelves, unread, for who-knows-how-long, with the rest.

Why make them guess?

But, oh, the treasures! Don't assume that your loved ones will remember what that painting means to you, and why it has always hung on your dining room wall. Or that your grandfather made that desk with his own hands and tools.

Don't make them guess which things were important to you when you're gone. Tell the stories of your special possessions to distinguish them from everyday objects, so no one is forced to rely on their own sketchy childhood memories when the time comes that you are no longer able tell them.

What is it worth?

Value is in the eye of the beholder. Sometimes my clients think the things they are saving, or the things they have inherited, are worth a lot of money. Usually, the things turn out to be worth disappointingly little. Occasionally, though, there's a valuable or sentimental piece worth giving some extra attention. If you've had it appraised, and know its value, make sure someone else knows about it too.

Meanwhile, the importance of a thing can be completely independent of monetary value. If they knew the stories behind your special items, your loved ones might be more likely to keep them, or more able to find appropriate homes for them. And, if they really do have monetary value, they'll know to try to sell them at a good price if they don't want to keep them.

Renewed enjoyment

As you select the things that have meaning to you, and tell their stories, you may find yourself wanting to use them more often, display them more prominently, and store them in a more thoughtful manner. In this way, you get to enjoy them, and they become even more meaningful.

PHOTO STORY:
Mom's Punch Bowl

Photo Credit:

Hazel Thornton

The Photo:

Flowers, fruit, and nuts on a kitchen counter

The Story:

The taller bowl with the ridged edges was my mom's crystal punch bowl. She gave it to me specifically, along with a set of matching crystal cups, not long before we knew she was dying. (I believe she suspected it at the time, though.) I remember her using the bowl and cups for punch at parties in the 1960s and 70s. But I've loved using the punch bowl as a fruit bowl (although, in the moment pictured I was using it for pecans). When am I ever going to make punch? (Well, when's the last time *you* made punch?) Still, the punch bowl is special to me. The other bowl means nothing to me, and I don't care what you do with it when I'm gone.

(This story is included in my Org4life.com blog post: *Are your keepsakes a legacy or a liability?*)

5 questions to ask yourself

(before organizing your memorabilia)

The terms *keepsakes* and *memorabilia* are often used interchangeably. They both refer to things we don't need for daily living, but which remind us of something or someone from our past.

- **Memorabilia:** Objects kept for their historical interest, especially those associated with memorable people or events. These can be inherited or collected from our own lifetime of experiences.

- **Keepsakes:** Items kept in memory of whoever gave or originally owned them.

Not all keepsakes and memorabilia are created equal. Remember: If everything is special, then nothing is special.

First, ask yourself these 5 questions.

If your collection of memorabilia is out of control, and you are wondering how to manage it, here are the questions I want you to ask yourself before you even get started.

QUESTION 1: Why am I doing this?

What is your goal? Are you organizing your memorabilia because you want to:

- Downsize in preparation for a move? (Is it a hard, imminent deadline? Or do you have time for a leisurely, more enjoyable organizing project?)
- Create more space in your current home?
- Simplify your current lifestyle?
- Make it easier for your loved ones to deal with your stuff when you die?
- Make money by selling items you no longer want to keep?

- Share the memories with your family? (Why keep the memories to yourself if you're the one who is in possession of them?)

- Leave a family history legacy for future generations?

QUESTION 2: Why am I doing this *now*?

How long has it been since you dealt with your memorabilia? How much space does your collection occupy? Are you having trouble finding what you want to look at, display, use, or share?

If you've inherited someone else's memorabilia, do you even know what's in those boxes? Are you ready to take a hard look at them? It's OK if you aren't. Take your time. There's no rush. Unless, of course, you're downsizing to move. Or you're in the process of estate planning and getting your affairs in order. Or you want to share the items with your family sooner than later. Or the boxes have been sitting there silently nagging at you.

But don't wait 16 years, as I did with my mom's 33 boxes of scrapbooks, photo albums, and other memorabilia! And don't store them in a dusty or non-climate-controlled garage, or attic, or shed, as I confess that I did!

QUESTION 3: Why am I keeping this?

You will ask yourself this question again and again, for each item you encounter. But, for now, just think about the overall quantity and quality of your memorabilia. And, as always, consider this: What is your clutter costing you in time, space, money, and energy?

Are you keeping it:
- To use, display, share and enjoy?
- Out of guilt or obligation?
- Because you don't know what else to do with it?
- Because you're afraid you'll forget the person, event, or era? (I promise you won't!)

We think of memories as priceless, irreplaceable, close to the heart, and hard to release. But not all the things we own, or the things left behind by a loved one, are valuable or important.

If you worry about offending a family member by getting rid of something you inherited, ask them if they want it. Or get rid of it surreptitiously. Would your deceased loved one want to see you suffer? Would they want your home to be cluttered, worrisome, and unlivable? Of course not! They would want you to feel happy, and to cherish their memory; not to feel guilty or burdened by them.

Once you've gathered everything that you have to remember them by, it will be easier to select a few special items and give yourself permission to let the rest go.
If your family or loved one is famous, you have an excuse to keep everything or donate it all to a museum or archive. Otherwise, as comedian Steven Wright says, "You can't have everything. Where would you put it?"

QUESTION 4: What will others do with my memorabilia when I die?

If you have been dealing with inherited memorabilia, like I have, you know how overwhelming the experience can be. Now is the time to start thinking about your own stuff. What are *you* leaving behind for others to deal with? Someone is going to be grieving for you someday; do you want to pile a heap of clutter and difficult decisions on top of that?

Do your family a favor: Downsize and declutter now so your family doesn't have to do it for you when you're gone.

If something is special to you, and you want the people you leave behind to know it, you need to tell them. And if you told them 20 years ago, you can't expect them to remember. Instead, use what you are learning in this book. Take a photo of the item; write a story about it; and let people know what it meant to you, otherwise it will get lumped in with the dishtowels and they won't know if it was important to you or not.

WARNING: This project may cause you to re-think the way you live your life! The more you keep in mind how you want to live your life now, and how difficult it is to go through your own memorabilia, much less someone else's, the more you will make mindful choices about what to acquire and keep now and going forward.

QUESTION 5: Do I need help?

It has been a little tricky being both the organizer and the client for my own project. For one thing, I didn't realize

that my mom's boxes would contain so much of *her* parents' memorabilia. There are some treasures in there, to be sure, such as my grandparents' love letters, but there's SO MUCH OF IT. But if I don't deal with it, who will?

I find myself getting distracted from the organizing task at hand the same way my clients do. And I give myself the same advice: "Don't read the letters now! Put them in the LETTERS pile. You can read them later!" I'm not paying myself for my time, though, so sometimes I go ahead and read the letters. Why not? The project is important, but there's no rush to complete it.

Fortunately, I had my brother's help with the initial sorting process. We've had to make some decisions for our other brothers who, also fortunately, trust us to make them. There have been touching moments, and funny ones. We've experienced a variety of emotions, ranging from nostalgia over our own childhood photos, to discomfort from reading Mom's private journals, to the joy of hearing her voice and her piano music on cassette tapes.

If you don't want to do it alone, ask a friend or relative to help you. If you don't have anyone you're comfortable asking, or if you suspect they'll be more of a distraction than a help, call a professional organizer to help you. *(See: Knowledge, Inspiration & Assistance)*

Ready to get started?

Now that you have answered the 5 questions for yourself, you should have a much better idea of where you are going with your project and how to get there.

Enjoy the journey!

Sorry, your kids don't want your stuff

One of the things I hear a lot from my clients is, "I'm saving that for my kids." If the kids are adults, I reply, "That's nice. Do they want it, though? Are you sure? Ask them."

If I had a nickel for every article I've read about "kids these days" not wanting their parents' stuff, and for every client who's confirmed as much, I could retire! But did kids ever want their parents' stuff? Maybe they did, but young adults today are more mobile, and occupy smaller living spaces, than in previous generations. This makes lugging familial furnishings around less appealing, even if it's something they like. Which, for the most part, they don't.

People who call me to help them declutter, or downsize before a move, often have a hard time parting with their possessions, even large pieces of furniture that are crowding their living spaces. They are especially reluctant to part with "valuable" keepsakes. (Valuable in what way – financially? historically? sentimentally? Valuable to whom – you? your family? a potential buyer?)

Well, it's true that your children might want *some* of it. But I'll bet they won't want *all* of it. *(See: PHOTO STORY: Mom's Good Silverware)*

Consider the age of your offspring. If they are minors, then by all means wait until they are mature enough to decide for themselves. But if they are fully grown and flown, with homes and families of their own, they will know if they want something or not. No need to store it in your garage for them!

The same goes for the stuff they left behind when they moved out. They either don't want it — ask them! — or it has just been easier for them to leave it there than to deal with it. If it's cramping your current lifestyle, though — perhaps you'd like to use that space for a home gym or craft room? — give them a deadline for taking it home.

You have the photos, the memories, and the stories. You don't need the clutter.

PHOTO STORY: Mom's Good Silverware

Photo credit:
Hazel Thornton

The Photo:

Some old silverplate serving utensils

The Story:

My mom directed me, on her deathbed, in 2001, to give her "good silverware" to my niece, Vinca — who was four years old at the time — when she got married. As an aunt, I wanted Vinca to cherish the set of Oneida Grenoble Prestige silverplate flatware place settings for 12 with extra teaspoons and serving utensils, use it, and pass it down to her own children. As a professional organizer, though, I was worried she wouldn't like it or want to keep it, as happens with so many adult children today. They have their own homes, and their own possessions, and don't want their lives to be cluttered with guilt-laden hand-me-downs. I wrote to Vinca in 2019, several months before her wedding day, to ask her if she wanted it. Then I waited with bated breath for her reply. The rest of the story is on my website, but — spoiler alert — *she said yes!* A happy outcome, but not a foregone conclusion

(A longer version of this story appears in my Org4life.com blog post: *Mom's Boxes Part 9: Mom's Good Silverware.*)

Part 5:
Be Resourceful

*The ultimate resource
is resourcefulness.*

— *Tony Robbins*

Why be resourceful?

Resources abound in the world of photos, organizing, genealogy, storytelling, memorabilia, and legacies! The ones I have mentioned throughout this book are some of the best and most reliable at this time. I have no financial interest in any of them; I just like them a lot. I have used most of them myself, and the few I haven't tried are recommended highly by my colleagues.

Please note that just because I may not have mentioned *your* favorite tool, app, blogger, or system doesn't mean it's no good! The best resources are the ones that serve our purposes and that we use regularly.

Let's look at some different types of resources:

Tools & Apps

Compiling these for a book is like herding cats (or maybe frogs) because they are constantly (albeit slowly, and usually with ample warning) improving, leapfrogging each other, changing their terms of service, merging with one another, and yes, sometimes hopping off into the woods and disappearing altogether.

Books, Blogs, and Podcasts

These are my sources of knowledge and inspiration! *(See: Knowledge, Inspiration & Assistance)*

Special interest groups

These include social media topic-specific groups, local clubs, historical societies, and software user groups.

Service providers

Many authors, bloggers, and podcasters also provide services to individuals, such as photo organizing and genealogy research, until, that is, they retire or switch gears.

Professional societies are usually regional or national, and more long-lived than the individual service providers of which they are composed. But they, too, sometimes disband or change directions, names, and website addresses.

(See: Knowledge, Inspiration & Assistance)

I don't want to discourage you by highlighting the ephemeral nature of resources, though. Don't worry, there will always be a way to find what you need. It might not be what you originally thought you wanted, but it might be even better!

Resourcefulness (creativity and problem-solving ability) is something we all have. And the more we exercise our resourcefulness "muscle", the stronger it gets.

Are you ready to find some resources?

Let's get started! The next section will tell you how.

How to find resources

Finding resources is like everything else in this book — the actions you take will depend on your desired goals.

Low effort *(Do this if nothing else.)*

- Locate the Resource Roundups tab on my website, Org4life.com. The listings there include clickable links that are updated as necessary. If you find a broken link there, please let me know! *(See: Org4life Resources)*

Medium effort *(Your family will thank you.)*

- Search online for any product, tool, service provider, or topic I have mentioned in this book.
- *See: Internet Search Tips*

High effort (*Ask for help if you need it.*)

- If you are on a website and you can't find what you are looking for there, contact the website owner and ask them about it. They are usually happy to point you in the right direction. I know I am!

Internet search tips

Do you sometimes have trouble getting good results from a Google search (or, from another search engine)? You are not alone! Here are some tactics to help you find what you are looking for.

Try different keywords

Think of keywords or phrases to describe what you are looking for in a different or more specific way. For example, instead of *photo organizing*, try *photo restoration* or *photo scanning*. Instead of (or in addition to) *archival quality*, try the terms *acid free* or *photo safe*.

Find out what's on a website

Many websites and blogs have tools to help you find out what content is available to you, such as a directory, search box, or list of blog categories.

If you don't see a search box, try typing this formula into your browser search bar:

Site:URL keyword

Note that there are no spaces between *Site*, colon, and *URL* (Unified Record Locator, or web address). Also, do not use the "http://www" portion of the URL. The keyword can be one word, or a phrase with quotation marks around it.)

Examples:
- Site:Org4life.com genealogy
- Site:Org4life.com photo* (The asterisk is called a *wild card*. In this case, it helps you find all keywords that start with *photo*, such as *photo, photos, photograph, photographer*, etc.)
- Site:Org4life.com "Mom's Boxes" (A phrase, such as the name of a blog series, needs quotation marks around it to narrow down the results from all instances of the words *mom's* and *boxes*.)

Narrow down your search results
If you are looking for a photo organizer (that is, a person to help you organize your photos, as opposed to a box

that holds photos in an organized manner), and you get an overwhelming number of results, try this method of narrowing it down:

- First attempt: Searching for *photo organizer* yields 254,000,000 results. That's because you are getting every instance of the word *photo* AND every instance of the word *organizer* on the internet.
- Now, add your location: Searching for *photo organizer Albuquerque* yields 913,000 results. So, you've narrowed down the results, but there are still an awful lot of them!
- Add quotation marks to denote phrases: *"photo organizer" Albuquerque* yields 37,400 results — you're getting closer!
- Use the minus sign to eliminate results containing certain words: *"Photo organizer" Albuquerque -store -box -album* yields 218 results. At this point you are likely to be seeing the best service provider candidates for your project, in your area, on the first page or two of results.

Broken links

Anytime you find a broken link (404 error code) try searching for the name of the product, tool, service provider, or topic to see if it has simply been moved to a different URL.

Remember: Everything is searchable!

Knowledge, inspiration & assistance

This list of authors, bloggers, podcasters, instructors, and service providers doubles as a personal gratitude list for the knowledge, inspiration, and assistance they provide to me on a regular basis! They are all in the business of helping people reach their family history, photo, and organizing goals, while making it all seem easier and more fun.

Maureen Taylor, The Photo Detective

(maureentaylor.com) She's the one who helped me analyze the photo of my bathing beauty grandma in the introduction to this book!

Cathi Nelson, author of *Photo Organizing Made Easy*
(cathinelson.com) Cathi is also the founder of The Photo Managers (thephotomanagers.com).

Lisa Lisson, Are You My Cousin?
(lisalisson.com) Lisa provides "resources and tools to confidently research your genealogy," including analyzing and organizing old family photos.

Caroline Guntur, Organizing Photos
(organizingphotos.net) Caroline, a.k.a. The Swedish Organizer, says she "lives at the intersection of family history and digital organization." She inspired the title of this book by once opening a lecture with the question: "What's a photo without the story?" What, indeed?!

Andi Willis, Good Life Photo Solutions
(goodlifephotosolutions.com) Andi is dedicated to preserving and protecting your family's memories.

Thomas MacEntee, Genealogy Bargains
(genealogybargains.com) Check out his free genealogy cheat sheets. And look for his excellent presentations at genealogy events.

Crista Cowan, The Barefoot Genealogist

(cristacowan.com) Crista is the corporate genealogist at Ancestry.com. If a webinar sounds like too much of a viewing commitment for you, try her new "Genealogy in a Minute" YouTube series.

Cyndi Ingle, Cyndi's List

(cyndislist.com) This website is a free, comprehensive, categorized, and cross-referenced list of links that point you to genealogical research sites online. I've been using it since its debut, more than 25 years ago! Cyndi is also an admin for The Genealogy Squad Facebook Group.

Amy Johnson Crow, Modern Genealogy Made Easy

(amyjohnsoncrow.com) The name says it all. I enjoy her podcast, blog, and Facebook group posts.

Janine Adams, Organize Your Family History

(organizeyourfamilyhistory.com) Janine helps amateur genealogists stay focused and happy while exploring their roots. She also co-hosts, with life coach Shannon Wilkinson, Getting to Good Enough, "a podcast to help you let go of perfectionism so you can do more of what you love." (gettingtogoodenough.com)

National Association of Productivity and Organizing Professionals (NAPO) (napo.net) Search for providers by zip code. Specialties that are relevant to this book include photography/memorabilia/collections, digital organizing, downsizing, home inventories, estate management, and more.

The Photo Managers (TPM) (thephotomanagers.com) Find a photo organizing pro, become a pro, or Do-it-Yourself.

Association of Professional Genealogists (APG) (apgen.org) Search for assistance by specialty, region, time period, and other criteria.

Personal Historians Facebook Group (www.facebook.com/groups/452415791769411) This is a private group, but they welcome inquiries from potential clients and from those who want to learn how to tell the story of their life.

If you contact one of these wonderful resources, tell them I sent you!

Org4life resources

ere's what you will find on Org4life.com, the website for my business, Organized for Life and Beyond.

- **The Getting Organized for Life Blog** includes longer versions of some of the photo stories in this book. Just search for keywords and phrases like *Gangster Hideout, Family Resemblances,* and *Mom's Boxes* (an ongoing series).

- **Resource Roundups**, including up-to-date links for most of the resources mentioned in this book:
  - Legacy Resource Roundup
  - Genealogy Resource Roundup
  - Photo & Memorabilia Resource Roundup
  - Emergency Preparedness Resource Roundup

- **Clutter Flow Charts** — 17 to choose from, including some that are pertinent to this book:
  - Original Clutter
  - Ancestry Clutter
  - Photo Clutter
  - Keepsake Clutter
- **Family History Services**
  - Genealogy Project
  - DIY with Coaching

Acknowledgements

My heartfelt appreciation goes to the following people:

- Everyone listed in the "Knowledge, inspiration, & assistance" resource section of this book.

- Standolyn — for once suggesting that I attend a conference session on photo organizing.

- Don — for teaching me how to do traditional, pre-internet, genealogy research.

- Julie — for asking lots of questions and making me a better writer.

- Shawndra — for patiently coaching me on how to format and self-publish a book.

- Jane — for keeping me company in The Zone.

- Ellen — for being a good listener.

- Dana and Sherry — for showing enthusiasm about a complete stranger's new idea for a book.

- My friends, family, colleagues, social media followers, and newsletter subscribers who kept me motivated by telling me how much they wanted to read this book.

- Mom for leaving me with 33 boxes of scrapbooks, photo albums, letters. And Dad for not leaving me quite so many!

One more story 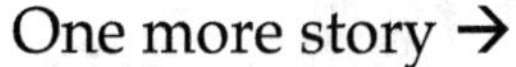

PHOTO STORY:
Breaking and Entering

Photo credit: Janelle Thornton

The Photo:

A young woman in jeans climbing over a fence

The Story:

This is me climbing back out of a locked cemetery, during a mother-daughter genealogy research trip to Tennessee, Kentucky, and Indiana.

Mom's photo album caption reads: "Hazel climbed fence to see markers in a second cemetery. Quaker, IN. 10-10-00." As it happens, October 10, 2000, was also her very last birthday. I'm so glad we took this trip together! Look closely — can you make out a few gravestones in the background over my left shoulder?

About the Author

Hazel Thornton lives in Albuquerque, New Mexico with 3 cats and the 33 boxes of scrapbooks, photo albums, letters, and other memorabilia she inherited from her mom. (And a few from her dad.) Ziggy, her office supervisor, was also her best pandemic Zoom companion. When Hazel is not writing she is researching ancestors for clients and for her own family. Or watching TV. Visit her at Org4life.com.

Hazel and Ziggy
(Zoom selfie)